"Shaker Church" (second Meetinghouse, Mount Lebanon, New York).
By twentieth-century American artist Albert Davies. Oil on canvas, 23½ x 17½
inches. Courtesy of Vincent Newton.

a YOUNG
SHAKER'S
GUIDE
to GOOD
MANNERS

a YOUNG SHAKER'S GUIDE *to* GOOD MANNERS

A facsimile of

A

JUVENILE GUIDE,

OR

MANUAL OF GOOD MANNERS.

CONSISTING OF

COUNSELS, INSTRUCTIONS & RULES OF DEPORTMENT,
FOR THE YOUNG.

BY LOVERS OF YOUTH

*" Virtuous Youth, gradually brings forward accom-
plished and flourishing manhood."*

PRINTED IN THE UNITED SOCIETY
CANTERBURY, N.H.
1844.

Edited by Flo Morse and Vincent Newton
with a foreword by Flo Morse

THE COUNTRYMAN PRESS
WOODSTOCK, VERMONT

*This book is dedicated
to all the young Shakers
who remained
in the faith and to those
who carried Shaker
values into the world.*

Detail from "Shaker Church" by Albert Davies.

Foreword copyright © 1997 by Flo Morse
Designed by Susan Surprise
This edition edited by Flo Morse and Vincent Newton, copyright © 1998 by
The Countryman Press
All rights reserved.

Library of Congress Cataloging-in-Publication Data

Juvenile Guide.
 A young Shaker's guide to good manners : a facsimile of A juvenile guide,
or, Manual of good manners, consisting of counsels, instructions & rules of
deportment for the young / [compiled] by Lovers of youth : edited by Flo Morse
and Vincent Newton: with a foreword by Flo Morse.
      p.   cm.
 Originally published: A juvenile guide. Canterbury, N.H. : Printed
in the United Society. 1844. With new foreword.
 Includes bibliographical references (p. 77).
 ISBN 0-88150-418-1 (alk. paper)
 1. Etiquette for children and teenagers. 2. Shakers—Conduct of
life. I. Lovers of youth. II. Morse, Flo. III. Newton, Vincent. IV. Title
BJ1661.JB   1998
395.1'22'088288—DC21   98-12026
                                    CIP

Published by The Countryman Press, PO Box 748, Woodstock, VT 05091
Distributed by W. W. Norton & Company, Inc., 500 Fifth Avenue,
New York, NY 10110

Contents

"*The Shakers of Lebanon, New York.— Sketched by J. Becker. A Shaker Schoolroom.*" *From* Frank Leslie's Illustrated Newspaper, *September 6, 1873.*

Come, little children, come to Zion;
Come, little children, march along.
And your clothing and your dress,
Shall be the robes of righteousness.

FOREWORD

by Flo Morse

COME, LITTLE CHILDREN, COME TO ZION

You must not allow them to be idle;
for if you do they will grow up just like the
world's children.

—Mother Ann Lee, founder
of the Shaker Church
(1736–1784)

You must take care of the rising generation:
for if they are protected, the time will come
when they will be the flower of the people of God.

—Father James Whittaker,
second leader of the Shakers
(1751–1787)

The Shakers are an American icon, famed for their "simple gifts" of music, craftsmanship, communal sharing and purity. They are the oldest and most successful of all the religious and social experimenters in American history. More than 220 years after Mother Ann Lee led a few pilgrims from England to establish the Millennial Church in the New World, the United Society of Believers still exists, though much diminished, today.

Less well-known than their other accomplishments is the Shakers' role as caretakers of children. Non-marrying themselves, they gathered into their communal villages from Maine to Kentucky large numbers of orphans and other children, many of them indentured by a parent or guardian. The Shakers hoped these young people would keep the faith when they reached maturity.

While they were growing up in the industrious rural communities, the children were very important to Shaker life. Not only did they enliven it, but they were productive and helpful on the model farms, in the busy workshops, and in the kitchens of the multi-storied dwellings. As adult conversions declined in the nineteenth century, the youth were viewed optimistically as future members and potential leaders of the church.

Within each "family" in the community, they comprised a Children's Order, separate from the adult Sisters and Brethren, who in turn were largely separated from each other, though equal in status. The girls occupied one house with a special Sister as caretaker, and the boys a different house, with a Brother assigned to their supervision and training.

For four months in the summer, when the boys' help was needed on the farm, the girls went to school in the village schoolhouse. In the winter the boys attended classes. Education was basic and practical. No useless knowledge was offered that would only "clog the mind and sense and shut the gifts of God

Shaker boys, and girls with their Caretaker at Shaker Village, Canterbury, New Hampshire.

out of the soul." Discipline, order, thrift, and obedience to the Elders, caretakers, and teachers were emphasized. So were manners and morals, as this *Juvenile Guide*, which was used as a reading book in many of the schools, details.

> When your superiors are giving you counsel, or reproof, never try to excuse yourself by the faults of others. . . . Take off your hat or bonnet . . . and stand up handsomely and still, with your hands folded: for if you hear and obey, it will be for your good.
>
> (No. 6–7, p. 94-95)

Always sit erect in company, not in a leaning or crooked posture, nor with your feet stretched out in the way of others; and be careful not to sit with your feet too far apart. . . . When you stand up, stand erect and trim, and not loll and lean against the walls. Be careful not to appear stiff, as though you were screwed up and in bondage.

(No. 14–15, p. 114)

But "growing up Shaker" (the title of a 1994 memoir by Sister Frances Carr of Sabbathday Lake, Maine) was not all duty and denial. Journals and daybooks tell of time off for picnics and sleigh rides, berry picking and nut gathering, ball games, and just roaming in the fields and woods.

"Us boys was down to the barn and we put up a swing and had some fun," wrote thirteen-year-old Delmer Wilson, a Maine Shaker boy, in his diary in 1887.

"Us boys" also milked and mowed, hoed and hayed, split and carried wood, raised calves, cleaned pens, picked stones, planted crops, and fenced pastures. They tapped maple trees, collected sap buckets, gathered eggs, shoveled snow, and mended shoes, among the many chores in the daily round.

But then one day, "Elder William said us boys might go down to the pond and we took the horse and snow plow and had a very fine time and when we came back, I went down to the barn and saw that Three-Tits had a calf."

Delmer refused to leave the Sabbathday Lake Shakers, as his brother did, when his mother came for them. He remained until his death in 1961, having long superintended the farm and orchard, made thousands of the famous Shaker oval boxes, and kept his diary.

Mildred Barker, who was brought to the Alfred, Maine Shakers at seven after her father died, "had a passion" for learning the old Shaker songs from the elderly Sisters who remembered them. She was especially fond of Sister Paulina Springer, whom she helped with chores. On her deathbed Sister Paulina asked the little girl to promise "to make a Shaker." Mildred fulfilled her promise. Years later she made the old songs a continuing tradition at Sabbathday Lake, Maine and was nationally honored for her contribution of music to American folk culture. She had been a memorable caretaker of Shaker girls, who gathered for reunions with her over the years.

"I don't want to be remembered as a chair," Sister Mildred once said in an interview, insisting that the Shaker heritage was its faith, not its collectable furniture. She died, a much loved spiritual leader and Trustee, at 93 in 1990.

"You couldn't explain the Shakers," Alfreda Hovey Beck said, admitting that she did not talk much about her childhood from 1906 to 1913 at Mount Lebanon, New York, home of the Central Ministry.

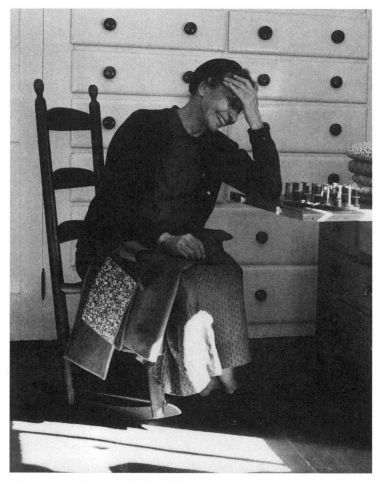

Sister Mildred Barker (1897–1990), spiritual leader of the Sabbathday Lake Shaker community, was once a beloved Caretaker of girls. Photograph by John Loengard, LIFE Magazine, © Time, Inc.

Late in life she discovered much interest in her experience. From the age of nine to sixteen, she lived in the Church Family, one of four families then still in existence at the community. At that time the families visited back and forth, and she remembered hearing the great pianist Paderewski when he was a guest of the North Family, and meeting artists and others from "the outside world" at the Second Family. The Shakers no longer turned away from "the world" as they once did.

Her special friend and teacher was Sister Amelia Calver, a progressive Believer who had been eager for "mind culture" and literary groups in the late nineteenth century. She awarded Alfreda good conduct cards for such things as "learning the Proverb well" and "darning her stockings so nicely." Alfreda remembered many good times, such as skating across a frozen pond pushing a straight Shaker chair, riding horses bareback, and holding the reins of a pair of black stallions on sleigh rides. She liked being swept off her feet by the long rope when she rang the bell in the belfry for dinner. She enjoyed the delicious meals at the long tables with marble tops. And she remembered marching around the meeting room singing hymns on Sundays, when the children took part in the services by reading from the Scripture.

"My years with the Shakers taught me forbearance and discipline," Alfreda, who lived in Vermont to the age of 97, wrote in a memoir. "Through their influence I learned to appreciate the basic, beautiful things in life. In some ways it was a paradise they lived in. . . . They did not dream of Utopia; they lived it every day."

Alfreda was privileged to run errands for a tall, illustrious, elderly Brother, Alonzo G. Hollister, who came to the Shakers at New Lebanon (it was called Mount Lebanon after 1861) with his parents and three brothers in 1838. He was growing up with ten boys in the Second Order when Charles Dickens called on the Shakers in 1842 to see their famous worship in song and dance. In an amusing account of his visit Dickens wrote that he pitied the young Shakers and did not blame them for "running away when they grew older and wiser."

But Brother Alonzo remained faithful until his death in 1911. He was an important communicator of Shaker doctrine, even corresponding with the Russian novelist Leo Tolstoy in the 1880s. In 1907 he had been persuaded to write his personal history by "a Worthy Sister, fond of books—especially those containing a record of the truths of our Gospel, and the experience of those who have lived it." In "Reminiscences, by a Soldier of the Cross" he described his youth in the Children's Order.

> The Caretaker of the boys had the care of the kitchen garden. The boys had to help plant potatoes & corn on the farm, also to hoe the crops after the plants came up, & to harvest

Boys in broad-brimmed hats with their Caretaker, Nehemiah White, at Watervliet, New York. A stereographic view, circa 1875, courtesy of the New York State Museum, Albany, New York.

them in the fall. They also had to help in haying
& harvesting grain. Besides our regular work in
the garden, we had to pick up the stones that had
been turned up by the plow, on the new seeded
fields that they might be mowed without striking
the edge of the Scythe on a stone.

Boys had to carry in the kitchen wood, nights &
mornings & also to keep wood supplied to all the
fires in the dwelling house, & the sisters shops,
during cold weather. Each lad, had one, two, or
three wood boxes to care for, during the winter.
In the dwelling house, the boxes were larger &
one box had to supply from three to five fires. A
boy had to help the herdsman, morning &
evening, & go for the cows & drive them again
to pasture. In winter, to chop roots, feed the
calves, pitch down hay, clean the stables, & such
other chores as boys can do. At this, several took
turns.

One had to feed the hens & chicks evenings &
mornings, & gather the eggs. These were our
regular chores, besides many occasional ones, &
the doing of errands.

But then,

Boys were allowed a play day, in the forepart of
Summer, to fish, or roam on the mountain—one

Boys pose at a well at Canterbury, New Hampshire.

Boys under 15 years of age are not allowed to go out hunting with guns; and the longer they let the guns alone the better.

— MILLENNIAL LAWS OF 1821

ride each, after they were ten years of age, to
Pittsfield or Washington, four miles beyond, with
the teams who went & returned same day with
lumber, & after 14 years of age, a ride with a team
to Albany, & return the next day. It was also
regarded as a holiday, to wander over the fields
together, with Caretaker, Strawberrying—having
our dinner with us—& returning so as to be in at
supper time. Also, to get up at 3 O clock A.M.
taking breakfast & dinner with us, & riding 10 or
12 miles to gather blackberries. Eating breakfast
at the end of our journey before we began to
work. The field of operation was deemd too
rough for the Sisterhood, but not for boys—
Riding home, the larger part of the way in the
dark—after filling our vessels—& supping on the
remnants from dinner. Boys were also allowed a
day in the fall to scour the woods & fields for
chestnuts or walnuts, all of which seemed like
seasons of releasement. Sometimes a whole day
would be spent riding—& others, boating on the
pond.

As the young Shakers like Alonzo and Delmer, Mildred and
Alfreda grew older, they moved into the adult dwellings and
assumed greater responsibilities. Side by side with consecrated
workers, they learned to do their work in Mother Ann's way—

as if they had a thousand years to live and as they would if they were to die tomorrow. Their jobs were rotated as the older Sisters' and Brethren's work was, and they took pride in the variety of skills they acquired. They learned how to grow and select the garden seeds Shakers were the first to package and which they had sold to the "world's people" since the end of the eighteenth century. They built the chairs for which the United Society was noted—straight-backed chairs, rocking chairs, chairs that tilted back on a ball in a socket, and chairs that swiveled. They gathered herbs and roots for the medicines of "the world" and for the syrups, extracts, and salves that were popular Shaker remedies.

The young women, taught that "good spirits will not live where there is dirt," scoured the rooms in the great dwellings and swept beneath the high peg boards that held chairs and garments. They helped prepare food for a very large family and flavored it with herbs and spices. They cared for the family clothing and made goods in the Sisters' Shops for sale in the village store.

On Sundays the girls marched two by two behind the Sisters, and the boys behind the Brethren, to the Meetinghouse, entering through separate doors, for the popular public performance of their worship. If the youth suffered self-consciousness before an audience of the world's people, they were soon swept up in the joy and drama of the sacrament. Dressed in their Sunday best—the girls and women in white gowns and the boys and men in blue coats and trousers—they moved from opposite ends of the room, with the singers in the middle, to dance in a throng in perfect rhythm, with symbolic gestures of their hands. Sometimes young girls would receive a "turning gift," described as whirling around with eyes closed "at the rate of forty to sixty turns in a minute," for as long as 45 minutes. (Brother Alonzo Hollister explained the phenomenon as "a willingness to turn out of our own ways.")

It was just such spontaneous whirling by teenage Sisters in a classroom at Watervliet, New York in 1837 that set off an explosive revival within Shakerdom called "Mother Ann's Work." The girls fell into a faint, and after they came to, brought greetings from the "spirit land" and tales of a heavenly visit. Other children were affected and soon adults had seizures, too. For the next ten years and longer, all the Shaker communities from east to west were flooded with spiritual messages, songs and dances, inspired drawings, prophecies and divine commands—all "gifts" delivered through mediums, young and old.

The children of that time enjoyed marching to secret "holy mounts" where imaginative ceremonies were held and visionary feasts devoured. There were also laughing meetings when the "laughing gift" was passed around until everyone was rocking in the straight-backed chairs or rolling on the floor. And there were exciting visitations of Indians and other "exotic" races, when Sisters and Brethren "possessed" by "spirits" went about whooping and dancing and singing in strange tongues. Because such

"The Whirling Gift," a wood engraving from Two Years' Experience Among the Shakers *by an apostate, David R. Lamson, 1848.*

. . . And then I first beheld the mystic dance; five or six women were whirling round on the floor with a velocity almost inconceivable. One of them continued this exercise, unabated, for a space of thirty minutes, without any appearance of dizziness or extraordinary fatigue. . . . Upon another excursion, I found forty or fifty dancing at once. The men were whirling around at one part of the room, and the women at the other. The room was much crowded . . . yet the holy ranks were not seen to break, nor the sexes to mingle.

— *"The Shaking Quakers,"* POEMS BY ST. JOHN HONEYWOOD, A.M. WITH SOME PIECES IN PROSE, 1801.

meetings were not for the world's people to observe, public worship was suspended.

Later generations of children taken in by the Shakers were never exposed to such a lofty degree of religious exaltation. And the "Lead," as each family ministry of two elders and two eldresses was called, worried as the years passed about the lesser commitment of the youth, despite their moral upbringing, to fundamental Shaker beliefs and traditions. After all, they had never been converted. Nor had they come voluntarily into a consecrated community to share its religious life and united quest for perfection. Yet it was essential to try to keep the increasing numbers of young people in the faith. By 1860 more than 25 percent of the population at the eleven eastern communities was composed of children under sixteen.

There were other bumps along the Shaker way: some running off, some restlessness, and some rebellion against strict orders and old-fashioned, repetitive rituals. Often promising youngsters were taken from the Society, sometimes forcibly, by parents or guardians who changed their minds or whose situations improved.

Moreover, even with the strict separation of the sexes, Church leaders were aware of the young Shakers' inclination toward the "natural affections." Girls, for instance, had to be reprimanded for parading about in the path of young Brethren. Brethren in 1834 were advised to set the candles for the Sisters outside rather than inside their lodging chambers, and the Sisters were told to fasten their doors. A young Brother recorded in his diary running to help put out a fire, aware that a Sister was leaning far out of a window of the Girls' House watching him with "her heart beating fast."

And so it was that eventually most of the skilled young farmers, artisans, and housekeepers reared with devotion by the Shakers went back to "the world" and "the flesh." Cities glittered, factories beckoned, and the Western frontier promised greater rewards than an isolated, celibate, religious life. Prayers to the Believers' Father-Mother God to "bind the young ones closely to us always" did not come true. Yet countless youths carried away lasting gifts from the quiet, picturesque communities, like brotherly and sisterly love, kindness, courtesy, thrift, neatness, industry, order, and simplicity—all of the attributes urged in this small book of instructions to young Shakers.

Despite the comings and goings of youth and children, apostates, and transients—including "Winter Shakers" who came in out of the cold and left in the spring—Shaker life continued serene and flexible into its third century. It has been estimated that in its long history more than twenty thousand—and possibly thousands more—Americans lived part of their lives as Shakers. In all there were twenty-five Shaker villages, only a few of them short-lived, in ten states. One remains, a small but active family of men and women at Sabbathday Lake, Maine.

This Society accepted children until the 1960s, and the village school served neighbors and Shaker students until 1950.

Sister Frances Carr, who came to the village as a child and is now the head of the community, remembers with a chuckle certain benign instructions. With the example of a bent-over Sister, the young girls were told, she says, to stand up straight "if they didn't want to be buried in a barrel." ✦

Little children are nearer the kingdom of Heaven than those who have grown to riper years. They are simple and innocent, and if they were brought up in simplicity, they would receive good as easily as they would evil.

Do not speak to children in a passion, or you will put devils into them. Do not cross them unnecessarily, for it makes them ill-natured, and little children do not know how to govern their natures.

— MOTHER ANN LEE

FRIENDLY CONCERN

TO THOSE WHO CONTEMPLATE PLACING THEIR CHILDREN IN CHARGE OF THE SOCIETY OF SHAKERS.

In consequence of the many applications to the Society to receive minors, and in order for those who place them there to gain a more correct understanding of the terms upon which they are received, it has been thought advisable to adopt the following rules and regulations:

It is to be distinctly understood by all who place minors among the Society of Shakers, that the whole care, education, government and management over them are surrendered to the Society.

No person will be allowed to make such minors presents of any kind, without the knowledge and approbation of those who may have charge of them; the Society at all time reserving the right to judge whether such presents are suitable and proper to be received by such minors or not.

All who visit such minors are requested to apply at the Trustee's office for permission to see or visit them, and not to go elsewhere, except by consent of those in charge at the office, and to conform to such regulations as may be deemed proper. In no case will any one be allowed to visit such minors alone, or in secret.

As the visiting of minors is attended with much trouble, time and expense, on the part of the Society, it is to be hoped that visits will not be prolonged to an unreasonable length, nor repeated too often.

Those who live within a few miles are not expected to stay more than a few hours, and those living at a distance, not more than one or two days.

Broadside, Shaker Village, Canterbury, New Hampshire, circa 1873.

*Shaker boy. Community unknown. Nineteenth-century photograph, gift of
Vincent Newton, courtesy of Hancock Shaker Village, Pittsfield, Massachusetts.*

A

JUVENILE GUIDE,

OR

MANUAL OF GOOD MANNERS.

CONSISTING OF

COUNSELS, INSTRUCTIONS & RULES OF DEPORTMENT,
FOR THE YOUNG.

—

BY LOVERS OF YOUTH.

—

IN

TWO PARTS.

—

" *Virtuous Youth, gradually brings forward accomplished and flourishing manhood.*"

—

PRINTED IN THE UNITED SOCIETY,

CANTERBURY, N. H.

1844.

A JUVENILE MONITOR.

CONSISTING OF

RULES OF CONDUCT.

FOR

YOUTH AND CHILDREN.

NEW LEBANON, N. Y.

1844.

PREFACE.

The following small collection of instructions was written for the perusal of youth, and such as might think it worth their notice. It is hoped that it may be of real benefit to those who have not had much experience for themselves, and who, like the bee, delight in gathering sweet from every flower.

Although there is generally no lack of good advice, and when it is dealt out with freedom, it is apt to become burdensome to some, yet a good remark will never come amiss to those who continually love the pleasant path of wisdom, and who are seeking to fill their minds with that rich treasure of understanding and knowledge, whereby they may shun many needless sorrows and troubles through this difficult and transient world.

That this little book may do some good, and no hurt, to its readers, and that happiness and prosperity may be their abiding lot, is the sincere wish of the WRITERS.

NEW LEBANON, N. Y., MAY, 1844.

JUVENILE MONITOR.

SECTION I.

Rules for behavior, in places consecrated for divine worship, and in meetings.

1. When entering a house, or any apartment devoted as a place of divine worship, always take off the hat or bonnet, immediately on entering the door, and conduct in the fear of God, sensing that you are in his holy presence. Laugh not, jeer not, neither be light minded or vain; but labor to feel a sacred reverence to that God whom you have assembled to worship, and serve.

2. It is disrespectful and irreverential to walk heavily, or flat footed; but all should walk carefully upon their toes, to avoid noise.

3. If the assembly unitedly sit, or stand, unite with the rest, if able in body; and either while sitting or standing, keep the body erect, and the limbs in a suitable and becoming posture : the hands decently folded, with the fore arm hanging about level with the elbows. it does not look well to see the hands folded upon the breast, or hanging much below a level with the elbows; It is also clownish to hang up the hands by the thumb in your bosom when folded; it discovers laziness.

4. The feet should never be spread widely apart, either in sitting, or standing.

5. If assembled in meeting for worship with those of the same faith, and at home, always unite in the worship, and not act the part of a spectator, either in singing, or worshiping.

6. Always devote the whole soul and every faculty of body to God, when assembled to worship Him, for this alone is fully acceptable in his sight.

7. Speak not, in time of sacred worship, of things common, or domestic, or any thing foreign from the duty for which you are assembled, unless necessity require it.

8. Let your countenance be moderately solemn, but cheerful, showing that you are delighted with your privilege.

9. It is ungodly and presumptuous, to feel, or speak slightly of divine songs, or any gift of God, however singular or strange it may appear.

10. In time of speaking, fix your eye on the speaker, but not gazingly ; and let it not wander to gaze on

any other person or thing; attend diligently to the words spoken, and strive to remember them.

11. It is ungodly to treat slightly or disrespectfully, the sincere devotions, in worship, praise, or prayer, of any denomination of professed christians, or any soul whatever, either professor or non-professor, although they may appear never so inconsistent, or improper to your understanding.

12. Always give attention, when you are in company with those engaged in prayer, either in meeting, or elsewhere.

13. It is very rude to play, while others are worshiping God.

14. It is ill behavior to talk, while others are singing.

15. Never presume to unite in the worship of God, while under the condemnation of sin unconfessed.

16. Strive to avoid noise when others are speaking, and be silent and attentive.

17. Seek to avoid coughing, sneezing, or blowing the nose in time of worship ; but if need require, carefully go out of meeting.

18. Yawning, looks sluggish in meetings for divine service.

19. It is indecent to scratch the head, or other parts of the body in meeting.

20. It is improper to wear dirty or ragged clothes to meeting ; thick, coarse and heavy boots or shoes are also improper to wear into meeting.

21. The person should be decently and neatly clad,

and the hair suitably trimmed and combed, before entering meeting.

22. All superfluous stroking or fixing, either of the hair or dress, for the sake of gayety, is hateful and improper; for whoever attends meeting for divine service, should be devoted to serve God, and not to the decoration of the person, which is ever wrong for the people of God.

23. Never go scuffing along, when exercising or walking; but lift your feet, and step squarely and properly.

SECTION II.

Behavior towards Superiors.

1. Remember that the way for you to learn good behavior is, to learn of those that are older, and wiser and better than you are. Copy their good examples, and yield strict obedience to their wise counsels.

2. Always mind at the first bidding, and not wait to be spoken to a second time.

3. Always pay due respect to your superiors; and when in company with them, be still and attentive.

4. When they are talking, do not be fond of asking questions, nor of putting in your judgment.

5. It is ill manners and very saucy to contradict them, or to argue or dispute with them.

6. When your superiors are giving you counsel, or

reproof, never try to excuse yourself by the faults of others ; but show respect and give attention.

7. Take off your hat or bonnet, (if you have one on,) and stand up handsomely and still, with your hands folded : for if you hear and obey, it will be for your good. Always thank them when they have done speaking.

8. Never keep your seat when your superiors stand for the want of one.

9. Never walk at the right hand of your superiors, nor before them when they are walking with you.

10. Never ask impertinent questions of your superiors, nor try to obtain secrets from them.

11. And when your superiors speak to you, and you do not understand, do not hollow out, What ? or What did you say ? But rather say, 1 was careless and did not understand ; or, I did not hear.

12. Never speak against your superiors, nor allow yourself to act against them.

13. Always respect and reverence the aged. Never laugh at them, nor mock them because they cannot walk sprightly, it is wicked. Always be kind and obliging to them ; for as you treat them, so you may expect to be treated when you come to be old. We will tell you a little story.

14. There was once a good little boy, who came where his father was at work making a trough. The little boy asked his father, who he was making that

trough for? "It is for your grandfather," said the father; "he is so old that he is not fit to eat with the rest; so I am going to have him eat in this alone."

15. The little boy said, "Father, shall I have to make you a trough when you get to be old?" His father immediately left making the trough, and treated the old man with kindness.

16. Now this little boy had not the privilege of being taught good things as you have; therefore do not let him excel you in goodness and respect.

17. Affront none, especially your elders, either by word or deed.

18. Always give the right hand to superiors when walking with them, or meeting them, and mind always to give them the wall side of the path in meeting them, or walking with them in cities; for that is the upper hand, although your superiors should then be at your left hand.

19. When three persons walk together, the middle place is the most honorable, and a son might properly walk at his father's right hand, when his younger brother walks at his left.

20. If children go with their parents, tutors, or any of their superiors, they should not go playfully along the way.

21. Refrain from talking with your companions, about your superiors, reflecting upon, or touching what you deem improper in their conduct; it shows an unbecoming forwardness, and cannot be said to be any thing better than evil speaking.

22. It is ill manners to run hastily by your superiors on meeting them, or overtaking them.

SECTION III.

Behavior towards Equals.

1. Never consider yourself above your equals; nor try to take the lead when in company with them; nor scorn their company and try to mate with your superiors.

2. Try to conform to your mates, and unite with them, (unless they incline to wickedness,) and strive to be agreeable in all things.

3. If the company you are in, do any.thing amiss, and you are with them in it, never try to excuse yourself, and throw the blame on others; but take your share of reproof.

4. When you want to ask a kindness of others, never ask them what their business is, or whether they are in a hurry ; but ask them handsomely for their assistance; and if they cannot oblige you, let them make their own excuses. For if you ask them if they are in a hurry, or what they are doing, it seems to imply, that you think such persons incapable of making an excuse for themselves.

5. Always be willing to take your share of disagreeable chores.

G

6. Never play mean dirty tricks upon any one; it shows meanness of heart, and an ugly disposition.

7. Never try to afflict those that are younger than you are, nor be fond of taking power over them unnecessarily. Be willing to have them in your company when convenient, and not show yourself too big to unite with them.

8. Be always careful to set them a good example, and never teach them any thing but what is virtuous and innocent; then they will have reason to bless you when they come to years of understanding, and you will have the pleasure of reflecting, that instead of corrupting their young minds, you have helped to guide them in the paths of virtue and innocence.

9. "As near as may be, converse not with any but those who are good, sober and virtuous. Evil communications corrupt good manners."

10. "Reprove easily and modestly your companions, as often as there shall be occasion, for wicked actions and indecent expressions."

11. Give place always, to him that excels you, in quality, age, or learning.

12. "Be willing to take those words, or actions as jesting which you have reason to believe were designed as such; and fret not, at your companion's innocent mirth."

13. Never give a joke, unless you can bear one as keen.

14. We ought never to say any thing by way of jest,

but what is short, and perfectly innocent; and never jest at all, only with associates or friends.

15. Finally, jests and jokes are edge tools, and very dangerous to use, lest we wound the tender feelings of our friends.

16. " If your companions be a little too sarcastical in speaking, strive not to notice it, or be moved at all by it; abuse them not, either by word or deed."

17. " Strenuously avoid sinful and unlawful recreations, and all such as prejudice the welfare of body or mind."

18. " Scorn not nor laugh at any for their natural infirmities of body or *mind*, nor affix to them, because of these infirmities, a vexing title of contempt, or reproach; but pity such as are so visited, and be thankful that you are otherwise distinguished and favored."

19. In speaking of others, in company with yourself, always mention *their name* first, whether superiors, equals, or inferiors; as, William and I went to meeting, not I and William, went, &c.

SECTION IV.

Behavior towards Inferiors.

1. Never call nicknames, or in reproving your inferiors compare them to that which you would dislike yourself; it savors of passion.

2. In making requests of inferiors, do it in the same

handsome manner you would have them do it to you. Remember, example teaches louder than precept.

3. Never speak diminutively of your inferiors in company when they do amiss, but wait until a suitable time, and give them a proper admonition.

4. Never allow yourself in that which is wrong when in presence of inferiors, thinking they will not know, or notice it; this will spoil their confidence in you.

5. Never make more free with your inferiors than you are willing they should make with you; it learns them to be saucy.

SECTION V.

Behavior at Table.

1. It has often been remarked, that it may be known whether a person is well bred or not, by seeing him eat only one meal of victuals; therefore it is highly necessary for all persons, strictly to observe the rules of decency and good behavior, while sitting at the table.

2. Always sit erect at the table, and not lean against it. The arms should be kept near the body, so as to take up no more room than is necessary. They should never rest on the table further than half way from the ends of the fingers to the elbows.

3. Be careful not to have your feet in the way of others.

4. The body should incline a little forward, when eating, to avoid dropping victuals on your clothes.

5. Spread your handkerchief in your lap, before you begin to eat.

6. Never begin before your superiors.

7. When you take bread, take your equal share of crust. When you eat bread, or biscuit and butter, take a whole piece, (if it is not too large, and there are pieces enough for all,) and lay it on the table by the side of your plate, and spread the butter over it; and not be cutting little pieces of butter and putting on your bread at every mouthful you eat.

8. Clean your knife on your bread before you cut butter, and after cutting it; or when your knife is greasy, before you put it into sauce, or cut pies, pickles or any thing else; but never clean it on the edge of the platter.

9. Cut your meat square and equal, fat and lean; and take an equal proportion of bone, and put it on your plate together with the sauce or vegetables whatever they may be; and not be cutting small pieces in the platter, and putting them directly into your mouth. Reaching over your plate to eat out of the platter is an indecent trick.

10. Be careful not to touch any victuals with your hands, only what you intend to eat yourself, whether you cut or break bread, cakes, pies or whatever; lest you leave the prints of your fingers for others to eat.— Nothing looks more clownish at the table, than to see

a person grasp and handle the victuals that he does not eat himself.

11. Never be putting victuals into your mouth, and at the same time be gazing round at other objects. And be careful not to be gazing round when you have done eating, before you rise.

12. Never gaze at a person when he is eating; for it looks as though you coveted his victuals.

13. Never plunge into the midst of a dish of victuals with your knife, or spoon, when you are eating minced victuals, or any thing that you eat directly from the platter or saucer; but what you eat, take out handsomely at the side next to you.

14. Never seize immediately on what you like best at table; nor eat sparingly of that which is common, and greedily of rarities; but wait until your superiors begin, and then eat no more than your share, unless your messmates leave it for you.

15. It shows low breeding and selfishness, to pick out the best of the victuals, or to turn over a piece of meat to look at both sides of it, before you take it to eat.

16. Never be squinting, and scowling, and examining the victuals, to see if you can discover a coal, a speck, or a hair; and if you do find one, take it out decently, and not make a great ado about it. For your honor's sake never make a mountain of a mole-hill.

17. A well bred person will never start suddenly and look over his shoulder, when any one drops a cup or

saucer, or makes any uncommon noise ; if any such accident occurs, he will never appear to notice it.

18. Always wipe your mouth, before and after you drink. Never drink with victuals in your mouth ; and be careful when drinking, not to extend the under lip so far out, that one would think the cup was going to be swallowed whole.

19. Eat what you need before you rise from the table ; and not be picking and eating afterwards. Never pocket victuals at the table, it denotes a thievish disposition.

20. When you have done eating, clean your plate, knife and fork, lay the bones you have picked in a snug heap by the side of your plate, scrape up your crumbs, and cross your knife and fork on your plate.

21. Scratching the head, or any part of the body, picking the nose or ears, belching, snuffing the nose, smacking the lips, picking the teeth, &c., are accounted awkward habits, and should not be practiced by any one who desires to be agreeable and honorable.

22. Come not at table without having your hands and face washed, and hair combed.

23. Sit not down before your elders are seated ; it is unbecoming to take your place first.

24. Speak not at table. Laugh not at table ; it shows unthankfulness.

25. It is ill manners to wipe the knife on a piece of pie, or cake, before cutting it off, to take on to your own plate ; but it should be wiped on a piece already in your possession.

26. " Eat not too fast, nor with greedy behavior."

27. Eat not so slowly as to make others wait for you.

28. It is ill manners to speak with victuals in your mouth.

29. Always keep the mouth shut while chewing; it is indecent so to open the mouth that others will see the food while chewing.

30. Stare not in the face of others while eating.

31. Grease not your fingers more than necessity requires.

32. Dip not your meat in the sauce.

33. Spitting, coughing, sneezing or blowing the nose, are all illmannerly at table; but if you cannot avoid coughing or sneezing, turn your head from the table, and put your handkerchief to your face.

34. If you have a cold, always clear your throat and nose before you come to the table.

35. Never raise phlegm into your mouth and swallow it at table; it looks very disgusting.

36. Stuff not your mouth so full as to fill your cheeks.

37. Blow not your food when too hot, but wait until it cools.

38. Hold not your knife upright in your hand, but sloping, and lay it down at your right hand, with the blade upon your plate, and the edge towards you.

39. It is ill manners to grasp hold of the blade of a knife when using it; you should take hold of the handle only.

40. Spit not forth any thing that is not convenient to be swallowed at table, such as the stones of plums,

cherries, &c., but, with the left hand, decently remove them from your mouth to the side of your plate.

41. Fix not your eyes upon the plate, or food of another at table.

42. Throw nothing under the table.

43. Look not earnestly on any one that is eating.

44. Gnaw not bones at table, (unless they be very small ones,) but clear them with your knife.

45. Hold not your bones with your whole hand, but between the thumb and finger.

46. Never drink with victuals in your mouth, and do not drink often.

47. When partaking of luxuries, consider whether there is enough for all who sit at the same set; if not, partake sparingly.

48. It is ill manners to pick the teeth at table.

49. It is very ill manners to clean the mouth with your finger at table.

50. Always pick your bones clean.

51. When you use a vessel that has a handle, always take hold of the handle, and not clasp round the vessel; it looks as though you did not know what the handle was made for.

52. When done using a vessel with a handle, never sit it down with the handle towards yourself, but turn it lengthwise, or towards the centre of the table, that it may be equally handy for all.

53. It is ill manners to be reaching over the plates of others at table, after that which is distant; but rather make some token of request for them to hand it to you.

54. Never put your fingers, or finger in your tea-cup, when you take it up to drink; but clasp round the outside, if your hand is large enough; if not, then take hold with both hands.

55. Never turn a vessel bottom upward at table, as a hint to the waiters you desire more of that kind of food; better call for it.

56. When eating at a nice table, or one which has a table cloth, never lay your bones and leavings upon the table, or table-cloth; but put them on the side of your plate.

57. It is doubtless the case, that most people habitually practice some traits of manners at table when at home, and in private families, which would not be considered by themselves, or the public, proper to adopt when eating abroad, with strangers, or at public houses. It is therefore proper to observe what is the custom of those with whom you eat, and generally conform to it; but there are some customs, however, which are manifestly improper. Such as leaving a quantity of food of various kinds on the plate when done eating; sitting at table an hour or two, and changing the dishes for every different kind of food, &c. &c.; these are the caprices of fashion.

58. Good manners require, that the plate be left clean of food and crumbs, when done eating, unless more is put upon your plate by your attendant, than you desire.

59. It is generally customary, (save in the private family meal, and sometimes there,) to provide suitable conveniences for the distribution of every kind of meat

and sauce, pies, custards, &c. &c. , which are upon the table; such as a butter knife for cutting butter from the roll or cake to put upon your own plate, and this is not to be used for any other purpose; in like manner, a knife to cut pie, a carving knife to cut meat, a spoon to the sauce dish, &c. &c.

60. All these things of course, are furnished to help one's self to such things with, as they are provided for; and such food should be removed by them alone, to your own dish. Although this is so simple a thing to learn, some, who would wish to be sure, to be thought well bred, do not seem to know it; but will neglect the use of these, when provided, and use those for such purposes instead, which have many times been put in their own mouths, which is very clownish, and ill bred.

61. In the social and domestic circles these nice provisions are not always made; hence some young people, before being much accustomed to going abroad, are apt, from the influence of their common habits at home, to make some wide deviations from good manners when abroad.

62. It is generally customary to cross the knife and fork upon the plate, when done eating, but for the better convenience of cooks, some families do otherwise. Customs differ in such things; however, it is generally proper in these respects to adopt the custom of those with whom you eat.

63. Eating quickly or very slowly at meals, is characteristic of the vulgar.

64. It is ill manners to turn grease or gravy from the platter on to your plate.

65. It is ill manners to cut bits of butter from the butter plate to put upon every mouthful or two of bread, potatoe, or other food which you eat, but spread your whole piece of bread with butter at once; or if butter be eaten with other food, take a suitable quantity on to your own plate.

66. Dip not your bread, or other food, into the gravy or grease in the platter; it is low breeding.

——

Supplement to the preceding Section.

1. It may not be a amiss in this place, to lay before our young readers, a short account of a certain person's behavior, who, it appears, did not exactly attend to the foregoing rules respecting behavior at the table.

2. Not long since I was invited to eat a meal of victuals with a number of people, among whom was a man by the name of LOW-BREEDING. I happened to be seated near him, on the opposite side of the table, where I had the painful task to notice some of his awkward habits.

3. As soon as he had seated himself, he seized the milk-pitcher and replenished his own tea-cup, and then sat the pitcher down by the side of his cup with the handle towards himself. I observed that he had finished this operation, by the time those at the upper end of

the table were fairly seated and had adjusted their pocket handkerchiefs. For his part he did not trouble himself with one; the back of his hand appeared to supply the place of a handkerchief, as I observed that he once in a while fetched it a wipe across his lips.

4. After using the milk-pitcher, he next made a dive at the meat with his fork, and, after turning a piece over once or twice to see if it suited him, he cut it in two in the platter and took the piece that suited him best.

5. While he was cutting his meat, I could not help pitying those who sat each side of him, for his elbows, which occupied almost as much room as a shoemaker at his bench, were nearly all the time goading their sides. I was some incommoded myself, for, besides his spattering the gravy almost into my face, his feet, I found were stretched out under the table as far as his legs would admit, so that they came nearly under my seat.

6. Next he helped himself to a piece of bread, by breaking off all the crust, and taking the soft part only. After hemming and sniffing, and glaring round and looking over his shoulder a few times, he began to eat; and now commences a most disgusting scene.

7. At every mouthful, he ran out his tongue nearly an inch, to catch the crumbs which chanced to fall from his loaded knife or spoon; and his lips were kept so far open while he was chewing, that one might easily see the whole process of mastication: though once in

a while he would fetch his lips together with a loud smack, which I took to be an indication that the victuals suited his taste.

8. When he drank his tea, he made a strange kind of a sipping noise, which I shall not undertake to describe. He eat so very fast, and took such large mouthfuls, that I was really afraid he would choke himself. However, when he had partially satiated his appetite, he stopped to rest himself by placing his elbows on the table and propping up his chin with his hands; and then, after belching a few times, proceeded again.

9. In the course of his eating, I observed that he had greased his cheeks nearly from ear to ear, and his fingers to the knuckle joints. He almost drowned every thing he eat in fat and gravy; and I believe would have sickened his stomach with the enormous quantities that he attempted to convey to his mouth, had he not dropped considerable of it on his clothes.

10. I shall not undertake to describe one half of his awkward habits and clownish ways, lest the reader should begin to think that I violated the rules of good behavior, by watching his movements. So I shall omit a particular description of many of his odd tricks; such as his mixing the different kinds of victuals together,— his cutting off the point of the pie and leaving the crust;—his grasping the cake with both hands, and twisting it apart, &c., and merely state, that when he had done eating, he left his knife and fork just where they happened to fall; his plate was covered with

crumbs and gravy, and as a token that he had done, he turned his tea-cup bottom upwards. When I saw this last trick, I could not help thinking of that bristly animal, which, when he has eat all that he can force down, roots the trough over.

11. In all the actions of Low breeding, there seemed to be a lack of that gracefulness so conspicuous in well bred people ; and he seemed to have habituated himself to rough and uncultivated manners. On my part, I was convinced, that he had never seriously considered that man in his uncultivated state, is unfit for society, and that he must have all his ways and manners refined, before he can be truly pleasing to those around him.

Table Monitor.

Gather up the fragments that remain, that nothing be lost.
                                                    CHRIST.

1. Here then is the pattern which Jesus has set ;
   And his good example we cannot forget :
   With thanks for his blessings his word we'll obey ;
   But on this occasion we've somewhat to say.

2. We wish to speak plainly and use no deceit ;
   We like to see fragments left wholesome and neat.
   To customs and fashions we make no pretense ;
   Yet think we can tell what belongs to good sense.

3. What we deem good order, we're willing to state;
   Eat hearty and decent, and clear out our plate :
   Be thankful to Heaven for what we receive,
   And not make a mixture or compound to leave.

4. We find of those bounties which Heaven does give,
   That some live to eat, and, that some eat to live,—
   That some think of nothing but pleasing the taste,
   And care very little how much they do waste.

5. Though Heaven has bless'd us with plenty of food :
   Bread, butter and honey and all that is good ;
   We lothe to see mixtures where gentle folks dine,
   Which scarcely look fit for the poultry or swine.

6. We often find left on the same China dish,
   Meat, applesauce, pickle, brown bread and minc'd fish,
   Another's replenish'd with butter and cheese,
   With pie, cake and toast, perhaps, added to these.

7. Now if any virtue in this can be shown,
   By peasant, by lawyer or king on the throne,
   We freely will forfeit whatever we've said,
   And call it a virtue to waste, meat and bread.

8. Let none be offended at what we here say ;
   We candidly ask you, is that the best way ?
   If not, lay such customs and fashions aside,
   And take this monitor henceforth for your guide.

SECTION VI.

Behavior in Company.

1. When you are in company, be careful not to talk too loud, nor too much.

2. Strive to appear pleasant, whether you have occasion to speak or not.

3. Nothing is more disagreeable than for a person to engross the whole conversation to himself; or, on the contrary, to come into a pleasant company and sit without saying a word, or even smiling.

4. Avoid telling stories in company, unless they are short and applicable to the subject you are upon; relate them in as few words as you can, and give the right meaning.

5. Avoid unnecessary repetitions, such as, says he, said I, and such like.

6. Never hold a person by the arm, nor detain him in any way, to make him hear your story out; for if he is not as willing to hear your story, as you are to tell it you had better break off in the middle; for if you tire him once, he will be afraid to listen to you a second time.

7. Never take another's story from him because you think you can tell it better; nor answer a question that is put to another.

8. Always look at the person who speaks to you, and pay attention and give a proper answer : for if you do not, it shows that you slight him, and do not think what he says worth your attention.

9. It is extremely rude and ill behavior to whisper in company, or to mock, or laugh slightingly at any in the company; or to be winking or squinting at some one, or to be jogging the one next to you with your elbow.

10. Whistling, drumming with the hands or feet, or getting up often to look out at the windows, and such like tricks, are indecent in company.

11. When you come into company where people are talking, never ask, What are you talking about? Who is it? What is it? &c. If it be proper for you to know, ask one alone, handsomely.

12. When you speak in company, in the praise of any person, never say, He is the best man that ever I saw; or the handsomest, or the wisest; nor use any such extravagant expressions concerning him; for this convinces the company, that you esteem the person you are praising above them. It is better to say, He is a good man, or a very wise man, or a handsome man.

13. Never go between two that are talking together ; nor run up towards others when they are talking to hear what they say.

14. Always sit erect in company, not in a leaning or crooked posture, nor with your feet stretched out in the way of others; and be careful not to sit with your feet too far apart.

15. When you stand up, stand erect and trim, and

not loll and lean against the walls. Be careful not to appear stiff, as though you were screwed up and in bondage.

16. Never allow yourself in any thing to offend your company, nor make any unnecessary ado if any of the company choose to smoke; but bear it patiently, or peaceably withdraw.

17. Strive to be still, when others are singing or reading.

18. Never allow yourself to nickname any one; nor to use vulgar expressions ; such as, hang it, plague on it, and the like; it shows low breeding.

19. Never be fond of asking questions in company, lest you show your folly and ignorance ; for those who are silent upon a subject that they do not understand, often pass as well as those who understand it; yea, a fool's silence often passes for wisdom.

20. Be careful not to promise more, nor boast of more than you can perform. For,

> " A man of words and not of deeds,
> Is like a garden full of weeds ; "
> Wherein no fruits or flowers grow,
> But such as are both mean and low.

21. " Put not your hand to any part of the body not ordinarily discovered in company."

22. " When you blow your nose, let your handkerchief be used, and make not a noise in so doing."

23. " Gnaw not your nails, pick them not, nor bite them with your teeth."

24. In coughing, or sneezing, make as little noise as possible.

25. If you cannot avoid yawning, shut your mouth, by your hand or handkerchief before it, turning the face aside.

26. Sit not with your knees widely apart.

27. Turn not your back to any, but place yourself, so that none may be behind you.

28. Read not letters, books, or other writings in company, unless there be necessity, and you ask leave.

29. Touch not, nor look upon the books or writings of any one, unless the owner invite or desire you, nor without liberty.

30. Come not near, when another reads a letter, or any other paper.

31. Let your countenance be modestly cheerful, neither laughing or frowning.

32. To look upon one in company, and immediately whisper to another is very ill manners.

33. When you treat a company with drink, fruit or food, always treat the elders of the company first; or if strangers are present, give first to them.

———

SECTION VII.

Behavior in Conversation.

1. " Among superiors, speak not until spoken to, or asked to speak."

2. " Hold not your hand, or any thing else to your mouth when you speak."

3. " Come not very near the person you speak to, lest your breath be offensive to them."

4. " Look not boldly in the face of your superiors while speaking, neither look some other way, but towards them, with a modest diffidence."

5. " If your superiors speak to you while you sit, stand up, before you give an answer."

6. " Speak neither very loud, nor too low."

7. " Speak clearly, not stammering, nor drawling."

8. " Answer not one that is speaking to you, until he is done speaking."

9. " Children should strive not with superiors, in arguments, or discourse, but easily submit your opinion to their assertions."

10. " If children should hear a superior speak any thing wherein they know he is mistaken, it is ill manners to correct, or contradict him, or to grin, or jeer at the hearing of it; but it should be passed over without notice, or interruption."

11. " In speaking to superiors, speak not without some title of respect, which is due to him to whom you speak, or, if he have a title, neglect not to use it."

12. " Mention not frivolous, or little things, among grave persons, or superiors."

13. " If your superior drawls, or hesitates in his words, pretend not to help him out, or to prompt him."

14. " Come not very near two who are conversing,

or speaking in secret, neither ask them what they converse upon."

15. "When your superiors speak to any other person, one side of yourself, speak not, nor hearken to them."

16. "If any immodest, or obscene thing be spoken in your hearing, smile not, but settle your countenance, as though you did not hear it."

17. "Boast not in discourse, of your wit, or doings."

18. "Laugh not at your own story, wit, or jest in any thing."

19. "Speaking of any distant person, it is rude and unmannerly to point at him."

20. "Be not over earnest, in talking, to justify your own sayings."

21. "Use not any contemptuous or reproachful language to any person, though he be very mean or inferior."

22. "Let your words be modest, about things which concern only yourself."

23. "Speak not over the words of a superior, that asks you a question, or talks with you."

SECTION VIII.

Behavior to Strangers.

1. Always treat strangers with civility and kindness; be careful to give them correct information, whenever

they enquire of you the way or distance to any place. Never be fond of asking their names, what their business is, where they are going, and such like questions; for if you do, they may see at once that you are not well bred.

2. Never stand and gaze at strangers; nor run to get out of their sight when they are coming towards you. It is very ill manners indeed, to stare and gaze at spectators, in the time of public worship.

3. Never laugh and sneer at strangers, because they appear singular.

4. Never go to the windows, nor stand in the doors to gaze at strangers when they are passing by. Be peculiarly guarded if the person looks or acts odd; for such persons often have as much wit as any; and if they see you gazing at them, they will readily suppose it is on account of their singularity from the rest of mankind; and perhaps will take the liberty to teach you good manners, by giving you a joke, or by shaming you in some way or other. We will here relate an instance of this kind.

5. There was a man riding by a house one day, who, from his infancy, had a very peculiar infirmity. His head, neck, and arms, were almost continually in motion, twitching in various directions; so that it made him appear very odd. This attracted the attention of the people in the house, and they all flocked to the doors and windows to behold the sight. The man readily supposed that they were gazing at him, on the account of his singularity, and thus cunningly

admonished them. He turned his horse short about, and rode up to the house and asked, if any body had died out of that house lately. He was answered that there had not. He replied, "I thought there was not any missing;" and immediately rode off, leaving the people to swallow the bitter pill as well as they could.

6. On entering a company where there are strangers, if at home, it is proper to address strangers before they do you, as a token of warm reception; but children, should always wait to be spoken to, by their superiors, whether strangers, or otherwise.

7. When addressed by a person with a compliment of enquiry after your health, &c., &c., always answer, looking at the person thus addressing you, and then return the compliment of enquiry, unless others of the company, have made the same enquiry before you; in which case, you should not repeat it, but evade the expression, by telling them, you are glad to see them, or some expression of welcome, or delight with their presence.

8. But, on returning a compliment, always call their *name* first, addressing them by their title, if they have one, if not, by the title of brother, sister, friend or neighbor, as the case may be. Thus, if a person speaks to me, asking how I do, I answer, and return the compliment, by saying thus, Elder Rufus, how do you do? or brother William, how do you do?' and not, How do you do Elder Rufus? which sounds improper; but much depends on the tone, which should be mild and pleasant.

9. When addressing gospel relations, it is proper to

use the title of Elder, Deacon, Brother or Sister, as the case may be. But when addressing strangers, not of the faith, it is proper to use the title of neighbor, or friend, as the case may be ; applying it, not to the given name, but to the sur-name, unless familiar acquaintance or near neighbors. But in addressing those who bear official titles, it is proper to use these on all occasions, when dealing with them in their official capacity.

10. Thus, if you had business of importance with the governor of the state, he should be addressed by the title of Governor, and if your business is not official, it may, or may not be done; but Believers in Christ's second appearing, make no use of the titles of sir, mister, madam or miss; nor of honorary titles; believing that titles of honor, belong to God *alone.*

11. When adults introduce a stranger, or strangers to company, it is good manners to introduce them to each individual, if the company be small, by telling the stranger their names, that he may know what to call the person, or persons unto whom he would speak;

12. But if the company be large, it is proper to introduce the stranger to the company collectively; and thus allow each one of the company to address him first, giving their names themselves, as occasion may require. For, should you introduce each individual to the company, it necessitates him, as a matter of course, to address the individuals of the company first, which would leave no chance for an exercise of propriety on their part, towards the stranger, leaving him to speak first.

13. But it is unhandsome and cool, to leave those who are diffident, alone while speaking to the company; better walk by their side, assisting them occasionally, to such little hints as may be necessary, for their information, and without a knowledge of which, they might appear a little awkward.

———

SECTION IX.

Cleanliness.

1. Cleanliness, is a very necessary accomplishment for all who desire to be considered as decent and honorable members of society. Slovenly persons are disagreeable to all around them; and contemptible even in the eyes of strangers.

2. It is in vain for any person to talk of purity of heart while he indulges himself in slovenliness; for filthiness of person and purity of mind, can never agree together. If the inside be clean, the outside will be clean also. Cleanliness of heart will show itself by works, as really as charity or love; and by their works shall they be known.

3. Always try to be neat and clean, in whatever you do. Be careful not to dirty your clothes more than is necessary; for it is a great labor to clean them. It is not intended that a person in order to be neat, should be a fop or a fribble. A neat, well bred person will freely

take his share of dirty, ugly jobs; but he will dress accordingly, and not dirty himself unnecessarily.

4. Always put your clothes on decently, and in good order; and never go slip-shod, nor with your shoes untied; nor with the corners of your collar tucked under your neck-kerchief.

5. It is a sure sign of a sloven to forget where you left your clothes; or to throw them on the floor or ground, or in chairs, and then sit on them.

6. Always clean your shoes well, before you go into a house, shop, or any clean place.

7. It it very indecent to spit on floors or stairs, or in sinks in kitchens; but always be careful to spit in the spit box.

8. A neat person will not neglect to wash his face and hands, and comb his hair when he rises in the morning; and will always see that his face and hands are clean before he goes to the table to eat.

9. " No one can please in company, however graceful his air, unless he be clean and neat in his person."

10. " He who is not thoroughly neat and clean in his person, will be offensive to all with whom he converses."

11. " A particular regard to the cleanliness of your mouth, teeth, hands and nails, is but common decency. A foul mouth, and unclean hands, are certain marks of vulgarity; the first sometimes occasions offensive breath, which nobody can bear, and the last is declarative of disgraceful negligence to remove the filth."

12. For black and dirty teeth, that are sound, there can be no excuse; they are marks of a vulgar, lazy

person. Let me entreat you, to clean your mouth every night, before you sleep.

13. It is a maxim which has been verified, that he who is negligent at twenty years of age, will be a sloven at forty, and intolerable at fifty.

14. The mouth and teeth should be scoured out once each day, with cole dust, which is not only good to cleanse the teeth, but is also an excellent preservative to them.

15. It is uncleanly, unnecessarily to get upon the floor.

16. It is indecent to lay candles, tallow, or any kind of grease, on a bench, or seat of any kind.

17. It is clownish to wear the hat on one side of the head.

18. It is uncomely to run about out of doors bareheaded.

19. It is slovenly to throw clothes, or hats on the floor, or on seats in a careless posture.

20. It is very slovenly, to wipe the nose or mouth on your sleeve, mitten, or glove.

21. It is indecent to look at one's handkerchief, after blowing the nose in it.

22. It is uncleanly to wear nice clothes about very dirty work, or very dirty clothes when engaged in that which is cleanly.

23. Always wash your ears, neck and feet as often as once in a week; and the washing of the whole body will not be neglected by cleanly persons, and in warm

weather, if engaged in dirty work it should be done weekly.

24. It is not tidy to wear clothes until they become very ragged; remember, a stitch in time, saves nine.

25. It is a sure mark of a sloven, to interfere so while walking, in muddy weather, as to daub the inside of the trowsers with mud, or wear them into rags.

26. It is slovenly to get on one's knees to build a fire, or to tie up one's shoes, unless required to by infirmity.

27. It is slovenly to leave clothes hanging up in, or thrown about in old buildings, shops, cellars, &c., &c.

28. It is not cleanly to put shoes or boots on the knees to pull them off.

29. It is improper to wear cleanly, or nice wearing apparel, with that which is worn about dirty work.

30. It is not nice to fold, and put away clothes into chests, cupboards or drawers, when wet, or sweaty; it exposes them to sour and mould.

31. It is indecent to throw dirty clothes on beds in lodging rooms, or else where, or on a clean seat, chair, or sofa.

32. It is slovenly to carry rubbish in your pockets, as bits of iron, nails, or any thing calculated to needlessly wear them out.

33. It is indecent to stuff the pockets very full of any thing which you are wearing.

34. It does not look well to go about with your hands in your pocket or bosom; nor with your arms folded; it shows an idle sense.

35. It is slovenly, to walk about the floor, in one's footing feet.

36. It is indecent to go about slip-shod, that is with shoes down at the heel; or with shoes untied.

37. It is slovenly to scrape the feet on the stove-hearth.

38. It is wasteful to wash shoes or boots to put aside, and allow them to dry up hard before they are greased.

39. It is slovenly to have several suits of clothes of the same quality, or kind, hanging about, or in wear at once.

40. It is very nasty to spit upon mats, or carpets, or in sinks, in kitchens or dairies.

41. Always wash yourself, when you rise in the morning.

SECTION X.

Useful Instruction.

1. Always remember that it is ill manners to peep in at windows, or to listen at doors.

2. It is ill manners to look over any one who is writing or reading.

3. A well bred person will never look to see what another is writing, without liberty; even if he should be writing at the same table, or have ever so fair an opportunity.

4. Never examine chests, drawers or cupboards that

belong to others ; nor read writings that you know you ought not.

5. Never go into work shops without liberty ; nor meddle with tools, nor with any thing where you have no business.

6. Always knock at the doors of strangers or neighbors.

7. Never go into merchants' shops, and ask unnecessary questions about the prices of articles, that you do not expect to buy.

8. Never be fond of asking questions when you go where others are at work, such as, What are you doing ? What is that ? Who is this for ? and the like.

9. Never be fond of gazing round and looking over your shoulder, when you are going through a city or village, or by a house ; if it is necessary to look, then stop and view handsomely ; or wait until you get fairly by, and then turn round and make a business of looking.

10. Never try to pester any person on account of his form, features or complexion ; for it is very mean.

11. Always thank a person who does or offers you a kindness.

12. When you offer any thing to any person, which has a handle to it, always present it with the handle foremost.

13. Never tell another that he lies, nor contradict him ; but rather say, I thought it was not so ; or, If it is so, I am mistaken.

14. Never cut and mark on furniture, casings, &c.

15. Be careful not to slam doors hard, nor walk heavy up and down stairs ; it shows a noisy sense.

16. Always be careful of books ; never hold the fingers on the print, nor double down the leaves ;—Never strain the covers open too wide, nor hold them near the fire, nor expose them to the sun; because it will warp them.

17. Be careful not to drop grease on your books, and always see that your hands are clean, when using a book.

18. The wicked borrow and never return ; but christians, and well bred people make it a rule to return whatever they borrow, as soon as convenient.

19. Always be willing to do chores and kindnesses for others ; in so doing, you will gain their love.

20. It is an old proverb, That children should be seen and not heard ; which signifies, that they should never be out of the knowledge of those who have the charge of them ; and when in company with superiors, should not be noisy and talkative.

21. Whoever has but one mouth and two ears, should remember that it is proper for him to hear much and speak little. A wise head makes a close mouth ; But,

> He that is a chatter-box
> And chatters all the day,
> Is like a bowl of milk that's skim'd,
> 'Till nothing's left but whey.

22. Finally, strive more to please others than to please yourselves, and strive in all your conduct to be

agreeable, meek and pleasant, with all your associates.

23. Be careful to regard the principles of honesty, punctuality and justice, in all your conduct; be neat, cleanly and industrious; observe the rules of prudence, temperance and good economy in all your works; subdue all feelings of selfishness and partiality; let the law of love and kindness govern all your feelings; shun all contention and strife, and be careful never to give nor take offence; conduct yourselves with civility, decency and good order before all people; then you will not only enjoy happiness yourselves, but will promote the happiness of all around you.

24. Always take off your hat when you enter a house.

25. "If you wish to speak with a person, either elder or equal, and see them engaged in discourse with company, draw back, and leave your business, until afterwards; but if you must speak to them, be sure to whisper."

26. Children should never grumble, or show discontent, at any thing their parents, tutors, guardians or superiors appoint or do ; and if any command or errand is given you to do, do it with cheerfulness, and alacrity. This shows a good disposition and agreeable character.

27. Bear with meekness and patience, and without murmuring or sullenness, all reproofs or corrections, although it should sometimes happen they are undeserved : But, being blameless, you may carefully take some other, and suitable time, correctly to inform the

H

person by whom you are reproved, how the circumstance in which you was blamed, was in truth; but be careful to do it in meekness.

28. It is ill manners to get onto a sleigh or wagon, without the driver's liberty.

29. It is ill manners to meddle with other's things without liberty.

30. Never hang round in company, where you are not wanted.

31. Never stand upon the sides of your feet; it runs down your shoes.

32. Never call nick-names, nor use by words.

33. Picking pockets, knocking off hats, throwing snow balls, clubs, stones or sticks in the street, or at each other, are extremely rude and vulgar.

34. Never play with fire or light.

35. Biting fruit which you do not intend to eat is improper.

36. It is ill manners to open a door and look into a room, where there is company, and go out without saying a word.

37. Always have a place for every thing, and keep every thing in its place.

> See ye not yon star of evening,
>   Shining through the verdant grove;
> Tranquil 'mid the gems of Heaven,
>   Gently blazing as it goes?

City of Peace Monday July 3rd 1854. I received a draft of a beautiful Tree pencil'd on a large sheet of white paper bearing ripe fruit. I saw it plainly; it looked very singular and curious to me. I have since learned that this tree grows in the Spirit Land. Afterwards the spirit shew'd me plainly the branches, leaves and fruit, painted or drawn upon paper. The leaves were check'd or cross'd and the same colors you see here. I entreated Mother Ann to tell me the name of this tree: which she did Oct. 1st 4th hour P.M. by moving the hand of a medium to write twice over Your Tree is the Tree of Life. Seen and painted by Hannah Cohoon.

"The Tree of Life." A gift drawing "received by inspiration" by Sister Hannah Cohoon, Hancock, Massachusetts, 1854. Ink and watercolor, 18 ⅛ x 23 ⁵⁄₁₆ inches. Courtesy of Hancock Shaker Village, Pittsfield, Massachusetts. Most inspired drawings were by Shaker Sisters.

ACKNOWLEDGMENTS

T he generous wish of Vincent Newton to share the instructions for Shaker youth in his *1844 Juvenile Guide, or Manual of Good Manners,* led to the compiling of this book. He also shares a twentieth-century painting by Albert Davies of the Mount Lebanon, New York second Meetinghouse, which has never before been reproduced.

Artist Davies signed his work with only his last name, and the list is long of those who helped track down his first name. Sincere thanks to Alan Price, George Schriever, Kara Short of Sotheby's, Jennifer Olshin of Christie's, and Lillian Brenwasser of Kennedy Galleries.

Warm gratitude is also extended to Sister Francis Carr, Brother Arnold Hadd, former Librarian Alexandra Regan, present Librarian Gay Marks, and Leonard Brooks at the Sabbathday Lake Shaker community in Maine; and to Director Lawrence

Yerdon, Sally Morse Majewski and Magda Gabor-Hotchkiss of Hancock Shaker Village, Pittsfield, Massachusetts.

As always, Melinda Yates of the New York State Reference Library was very helpful, as were Virginia McEwen of the Shaker Museum and Library, Magdalyn Sebastian and Craig Williams of the New York State Museum, Cathy Grosfils of the Abby Aldrich Rockefeller Folk Art Collection, and Debra Cohen of Time Life Syndication. Thanks, too, to Larrie Curry of the Shaker Village of Pleasant Hill and Jean Solensky of the Henry du Pont Winterthur Museum.

Among many informative headnotes in Dr. Daniel Patterson's book, *The Shaker Spiritual*, one about Brother Alonzo Hollister's youth at New Lebanon led to the original biographical material in the Western Reserve Historical Society Reference Library. Priscilla Brewer's profound research and conclusions in *Shaker Communities, Shaker Lives* must be acknowledged as well.

We are supremely indebted to Susan Surprise for designing our book with scrupulous care and artistry. And we thank others who contributed along the way, including booksellers Scott De Wolfe and Frank Wood, Librarian Ralph Stenstrom and photographer Marianita Amodio of the Hamilton College Library, Elizabeth Hancock, and Joe Morse. ✦

FLO MORSE
SANTA FE, NEW MEXICO

A Sister and two youngsters, in the 1870s, in a group on the side steps of the Centre Family House at the Shaker Village of Pleasant Hill, Kentucky. Photograph, courtesy of The Winterthur Library: The Edward Deming Andrews Memorial Shaker Collection.

Children under the age of 12 or 14 years must have their pie cut for them & laid by their dishes—Also, when they have bread & butter, suitable pieces must be properly spread & laid by their dishes.

— EARLY TABLE MONITOR

The instructions for Shaker youth reproduced in this book were based on an earlier manual of twenty pages published in 1823. Its title was: *A Juvenile Monitor: Containing Instructions For Youth and Children: Pointing out Ill Manners, and Showing Them How To Behave In the Various Conditions of Childhood and Youth.* It was written by the instructors of the Shaker school at New Lebanon, New York, who considered it

> a matter of very great importance that the young mind should be properly and carefully trained up in the right way, not only by example, but by teaching and admonition, and by reading such books as are suitable for them.

The instructors, according to the Library of Congress, quoted by Mary L. Richmond in Vol. II of her *Bibliography of Shaker Literature*, were Shaker Brethren Rufus Bishop, Garrett Lawrence, and Isaac Newton Youngs.

In 1844 the earlier book was revised and enlarged by Elder Giles Avery and named *A Juvenile Guide, or Manual of Good Manners. Consisting of Counsels, Instructions & Rules of Deportment for the Young.* A thousand copies were printed at Canterbury, New Hampshire by Elder Henry Blinn. A small book with brown board covers, it contains 130 pages and had a general circulation in the Shaker communities.

For "the better cultivation of the social civilities" and the "good graces of well-disciplined society," Elder Henry printed a third, revised edition at Canterbury in 1899 entitled *Gentle Manners*. In 1978 a reproduction of *Gentle Manners* was published at Canterbury, with a preface by Eldress Bertha Lindsay.

The present book offers Part II of the 1844 *A Juvenile Guide*. Through its prohibitions and admonitions it reveals a charming profile of the young people who grew up in the loving and particular care of the people called Shakers. ✦

∿ Greetings ∿

To YOU, from the Society of American Shakers, who, though living among you for more than a century and a half (1774-1937) and claiming the distinction of existing longer than any other Communistic order, are yet little known and less understood.

Communism,* though as old as history itself, seems never to have gained a foothold in any community except when identified with some religious creed, hence, the Shakers credit their long existence to the religious principles of their order:-
Virgin Purity — Peace — Justice and Love, expressed in a Celibate Life, United Inheritance, and Universal Brotherhood.

The first to recognize Sex Equality, Freedom of Thought and Religious Tolerance, the Shakers have found that "Peace that Passeth Understanding" in their Brother and Sister Relationship, realizing the while that Their's is the field for the few rather than the many, though open to all sincerely-minded persons.

Their motto, "Hands to work and Hearts to God" demands a life of Service, which finds fulfillment in the care and education of needy children (which may or may not remain with the Society when becoming of age) wholly by their own efforts, without any reimbursement by the State.

These children are early taught the art of handwork and the results of their efforts, when well done, are placed on sale to help in their support. Your patronage or contribution thus helps those who cannot care for themselves.

Let us ask you to sum up the Shakers life effort in the words of the well known poem:-
Do all the good you can,
In all the ways you can,
To all the people you can,
In every place you can,
At all the times you can,
As long as ever you can.

*Please do not confuse with Soviet Communism.

A broadside in behalf of needy children raised at Sabbathday Lake, Maine, 1935. (By Sister R. Mildred Barker.) Editor's collection.

THE SHAKER COMMUNITIES

1	Watervliet, New York	1787–1938
2	Mount Lebanon, New York	1787–1947
3	Hancock, Massachusetts	1790–1960
4	Enfield, Connecticut	1790–1917
5	Harvard, Massachusetts	1791–1918
6	Tyringham, Massachusetts	1792–1875
7	Canterbury, New Hampshire	1792–1992
8	Alfred, Maine	1793–1931
9	Enfield, New Hampshire	1793–1923
10	Shirley, Massachusetts	1793–1908
11	**Sabbathday Lake, Maine**	**1794–Ongoing**
12	Pleasant Hill, Kentucky	1805–1910
13	Union Village, Ohio	1805–1912
14	Watervliet, Ohio	1806–1900
15	South Union, Kentucky	1807–1922
16	West Union (Busro), Indiana	1807–1827
17	Gorham, Maine	1808–1819
18	New Canaan, Connecticut	1810–1812
19	Savoy, Massachusetts	1817–1821
20	North Union, Ohio	1822–1889
21	White Water, Ohio	1822–1916
22	Sodus Bay, New York	1826–1836
23	Groveland, New York	1836–1892
24	Narcoossee, Florida	1895–1924
25	White Oak, Georgia	1898–1902

Gymnastics at Canterbury, New Hampshire. Photograph, courtesy of Hancock Shaker Village, Pittsfield, Massachusetts.

Books of Interest

Beck, Dorothy, ed. *Exit 76.* "Shaker Memories" by Alfreda Hovey [Beck]. Lebanon, New Hampshire: New Victoria Printers, Inc., 1976.

Brewer, Priscilla. *Shaker Communities, Shaker Lives.* Hanover and London: University Press of New England, 1986.

Burns, Deborah E. *Shaker Cities of Peace, Love, and Union.* Hanover and London: University Press of New England, 1992. Published in cooperation with Hancock Shaker Village, Inc.

Carr, Sister Frances. *Growing Up Shaker.* New Gloucester, Maine: The United Society of Shakers, 1994.

Dickens, Charles. *American Notes For General Circulation.* Ch. 15. London: Chapman and Hall, 1842. Reprint, New York: St. Martin's Press, 1985.

Giles, Janice Holt. *The Believers.* Lexington, Kentucky: The University Press of Kentucky, 1989. (Reprint of 1957 novel)

Grant, Jerry V. *Noble But Plain: The Shaker Meetinghouse at Mount Lebanon.* Old Chatham, New York: Shaker Series, Center for Research and Education, Shaker Museum and Library, 1994.

Johnson, Brother Theodore E. "Notes and an Introduction: The Diary of a Maine Shaker Boy: Delmer Wilson—1887." *Shaker Quarterly.* Vol 8, No 1, Spring 1968, p. 3–22.

Kirk, John T. *The Shaker World: Art, Life, Belief.* New York: Harry N. Abrams, Inc., 1997.

Moriarty, Kathleen M. *Integrating Shaker Studies into Your Curriculum.* Holland, Michigan: The World of Shaker, 1992.

Morse, Flo. *The Story of the Shakers.* Woodstock, Vermont: The Countryman Press, 1986.

Murray, Stuart. *Shaker Heritage Guidebook.* Spencertown, New York: Golden Hill Press, 1994.

Patterson, Daniel W. *The Shaker Spiritual.* Princeton, New Jersey: Princeton University Press, 1979.

Pearson, Elmer R., and Neal, Julia. *The Shaker Image.* Second and Annotated Edition, with Annotations, Appendices and Index by Dr. Magda Gabor-Hotchkiss. Pittsfield, Massachusetts: Hancock Shaker Village, Inc., 1994.

Ray, Mary Lyn. *Shaker Boy.* (Juvenile) San Diego: Browndeer Press, Harcourt Brace & Co., 1994.

Rourke, Constance. *The Roots of American Culture and Other Essays.* "The Shakers." New York: Harcourt, Brace & World, 1942.

Stein, Stephen J. *The Shaker Experience in America.* New Haven and London: Yale University Press, 1992.

Thorne-Thomsen, Kathleen. *Shaker Children: True Stories and Crafts.* (Juvenile) Chicago: Chicago Review Press, 1996.

Wertkin, Gerard C. *The Four Seasons of Shaker Life.* New York: Simon & Schuster, Inc., 1986.

Wiggin, Kate Douglas. *Susanna and Sue.* (Fiction) Boston: Houghton Mifflin Company, 1909.

✦

Girls at Sabbathday Lake, Maine in 1942, in their new slacks but still wearing the upper portion of their Shaker dresses. Second from left in the first row is Sister Frances Carr, now head of the Shaker community. Photograph from her book, Growing Up Shaker, *from the Collection of the United Society of Shakers, Sabbathday Lake, Maine.*

Look not to the follies and pleasures of earth,
If you would inherit pure, heavenly mirth;
But travel in righteousness, meekness and truth,
And overcome all the temptations of youth.

— ANONYMOUS

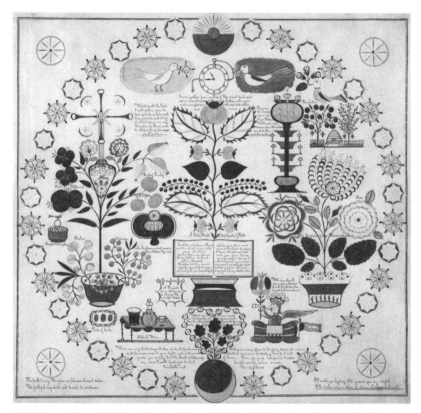

"A Present from Mother Ann to Mary H." A gift drawing *"received by inspi-ration"* by Sister Polly Jane Reed, New Lebanon, New York, 1848. Multicolors on pale-blue paper, 14 x 14 ¼ inches. Courtesy of The Abby Aldrich Rockefeller Folk Art Collection, Williamsburg, Virginia. Details on pages 77, 81, and back endpaper.

Shaker Museums,
Collections & Libraries

The United Society of Shakers
Shaker Residence and Museum
New Gloucester, Maine
207-926-4597

American Antiquarian Society
Worcester, Massachusetts
508-755-5221

American Museum in Britain
Claverton Manor
Bath, England
01225 460503

American Society for Psychical
Research
New York, New York
212-799-5050

Art Complex Museum
Duxbury, Massachusetts
617-934-6634

Berkshire Athenaeum
Pittsfield, Massachusetts
413-499-9486

Buffalo and Erie County
Public Library
Buffalo, New York
716-858 7118

Canterbury Shaker Village
Canterbury, New Hampshire
603-783-9511

Coastal Georgia Historical Society
St. Simons Island, Georgia
912-638-4666

Connecticut State Library
Hartford, Connecticut
203-566-4777 or 5776

Dartmouth College
Baker Library
Hanover, New Hampshire
603-646-2037

Dayton and Montgomery
Public Library
Dayton, Ohio
513-227-9500

Duke University
William R. Perkins Library
Durham, North Carolina
919-684-2855

Durham Tavern Museum
Cleveland, Ohio
216-431-1060

Enfield Historical Society
Enfield, Connecticut
203-745-1724

Enfield Shaker Museum
Enfield, New Hampshire
603-632-4346

Filson Club Historical Society
Louisville, Kentucky
502-635-5083

Fruitlands Museum
Prospect Hill
Harvard, Massachusetts
508-456-3924

Genesee Country Museum
Mumford, New York
716-538-6822

Georgia Historical Society
Savannah, Georgia
912-651-2128 or 944-2128

Golden Lamb Inn
Lebanon, Ohio
513-932-5065

Hamilton College Library
Clinton, New York
315-859-4479

Hancock Shaker Village
Pittsfield, Massachusetts
413-443-0188

Hofstra University
Axinn Library
Hempstead, New York
516-560-5097

Hood Museum of Art
Hanover, New Hampshire
603-646-2808

Indiana Historical Society Library
Indianapolis, Indiana
Historical Society: 317-233-1882
Library: 317-232-1879

Kentucky Museum and Library
Bowling Green, Kentucky
Museum: 502-745-2592
Library: 502-745-6086

Kettering-Moraine Museum
Kettering, Ohio
513-299-2722

Library of Congress
Washington, D.C.
202-566-4777

Livingston County Museum
Geneseo, New York
716-243-9147 or 2332

Massachusetts Historical Society
Boston, Massachusetts
617-536-1608

Metropolitan Museum of Art
New York, New York
212-879-5500

Milwaukee Art Museum
Milwaukee, Wisconsin
414-224-3200

Museum of American Folk Art
New York, New York
212-595-9533

New Canaan Historical Society
New Canaan, Connecticut
203-966-1776

New Hampshire Historical
Society Library
Concord, New Hampshire
603-225-3381

New York Public Library
New York, New York
212-930-0801

New York State Library
Albany, New York
518-474-6282

New York State Museum
Albany, New York
518-474-5353

Ohio Historical Society
Columbus, Ohio
614-297-2510

Osceola County Historical Society
Kissimmee, Florida
407-396-8644

Otterbein Homes
Lebanon, Ohio
513-932-2020

Philadelphia Museum of Art
Philadelphia, Pennsylvania
215-763-8100

Shaker Heritage Society
Albany, New York
518-456-7890

Shaker Historical Society
Shaker Heights, Ohio
216-921-1201

Shaker Museum
Old Chatham, New York
518-794-9100

Shakertown at South Union
South Union, Kentucky
502-542-4167

Shaker Village at Pleasant Hill
Harrodsburg, Kentucky
606-734-5411

Shelburne Museum
Shelburne, Vermont
802-985-3344

Shirley Historical Society
Shirley, Massachusetts
508-425-9328

State Historical Society of Wisconsin
Madison, Wisconsin
608-262-9576

Syracuse University
George Arents Research Library
Syracuse, New York
315-443-2697

University of Kentucky
Margaret I. King Library
Lexington, Kentucky
606-258-8611

Villa Terrace Decorative
Arts Museum
Villa Terrace, Wisconsin
414-271-3656

Warren County Historical
Society Museum
Lebanon, Ohio
513-932-1817

Western Reserve Historical Society
Museum and Library
Cleveland, Ohio
216-721-5727

Williams College
Sawyer Library
Williamstown, Massachusetts
413-597-2568

Henry Francis du Pont Winterthur
Museum
Winterthur, Delaware
302-888-4600

✦

A SHAKER LAD AND HIS SISTER STOLEN!

(From an account in the Portland, Maine *Eastern Argus* of a journey by steamboat and stage from New York to Springfield, Massachusetts)

AUGUST 30, 1847

At Pittsfield, I took the stage for Lee, passing Lenox, a pleasant village—the residence of Miss. C.M. Sedgwick [a noted author of the time]. Among the passengers, was a little chap, about twelve years of age, who had just been *stolen* from the Shakers at Lebanon *by his father.* His father and mother quit the Shakers last spring, leaving three of their children—two boys and one girl. Some weeks or months since, he succeeded by strategem in getting possession of his daughter, who is not more than four or five years of age. Providing himself with a swift horse and suitable carriage, he took an elder son with him on a pretended visit to his daughter. Asking to see her, permission was given to the father, while the son remained in the road near the horse and carriage. Having the child in his arms, caressing it, he seized his opportunity to escape with it to the wagon, into which he hastened with his prize and drove off at the utmost speed, without waiting even for his son to get in. His son remained out of the wagon, to act, if necessary, as a sort of rear guard in case of pursuit—which not being made, he had only to walk home by himself. On Friday last, the father being ripe for another like enterprise, he drove toward the village and had the good fortune to come suddenly upon his two remaining Shaker sons, with other lads picking blackberries. He immediately seized the younger, who screamed like a "new one"—as did the elder, who made good his escape. However, the captured lad soon became pacified, and on being placed in charge of our stage driver, declared he would never return to the Shakers, but was rejoiced that he was so soon to see his mother, brother and sisters again. The father, who is not yet an old man, is fully resolved on restoring his other son to the paternal roof.

Sometimes a parent refused to abide by the agreement to leave children with the Shakers. Newspaper item, courtesy of Librarian Ralph Stenstrom, Hamilton College Library.

From a gift drawing by Polly Collins, received at Hancock in 1853. Courtesy of the Library of Congress.

Come old and young, come great and small,
Here's love and union free for all;
And every one that will obey,
Have now a right to dance and play;
For dancing is a sweet employ,
It fills the soul with heavenly joy,
It makes our love and union flow,
While round, and round, and round we go.

— MILLENNIAL PRAISES, 1813